20 FUN FACTS ABOUT THE CIRCULATORY SYSTEM

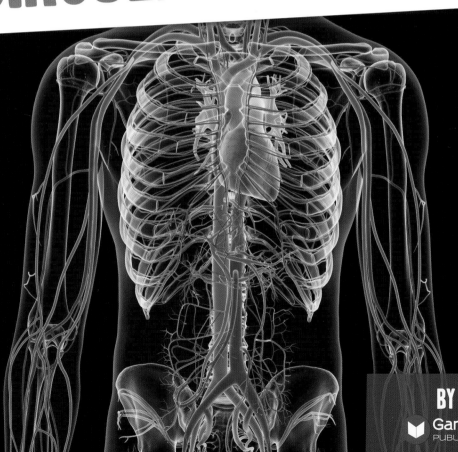

BY TAYLER COLE

Gareth Stevens
PUBLISHING

Please visit our website, www.garethstevens.com. For a free color catalog of all our high-quality books, call toll free 1-800-542-2595 or fax 1-877-542-2596.

Library of Congress Cataloging-in-Publication Data

Names: Cole, Tayler, author.
Title: 20 fun facts about the circulatory system / Tayler Cole.
Description: New York : Gareth Stevens Publishing, [2019] | Series: Fun fact file: body systems | Includes index.
Identifiers: LCCN 2018026462| ISBN 9781538229217 (library bound) | ISBN 9781538232729 (pbk.) | ISBN 9781538232736 (6 pack)
Subjects: LCSH: Cardiovascular system–Juvenile literature. | Heart–Juvenile literature.
Classification: LCC QP103 .C64 2019 | DDC 612.1–dc23
LC record available at https://lccn.loc.gov/2018026462

First Edition

Published in 2019 by
Gareth Stevens Publishing
111 East 14th Street, Suite 349
New York, NY 10003

Designer: Sarah Liddell
Editor: Meta Manchester

Photo credits: Cover, pp. 1 (main), 11 Sebastian Kaulitzki/Shutterstock.com; file folder used throughout David Smart/Shutterstock.com; binder clip used throughout luckyraccoon/Shutterstock.com; wood grain background used throughout ARENA Creative/Shutterstock.com; p. 5 Macrovector/Shutterstock.com; pp. 6, 8 Lightspring/Shutterstock.com; p. 7 yaruna/Shutterstock.com; p. 9 FatCamera/E+/Getty Images; p. 10 GoTaR/Shutterstock.com; pp. 12, 25 (background), 27 Nerthuz/Shutterstock.com; p. 13 Dan McCoy - Rainbow/Science Faction/Getty images; p. 14 Ed Reschke/Photolibrary/Getty Images; p. 15 Andrey Armyagov/Shutterstock.com; p. 16 Cheryl Casey/Shutterstock.com; p. 17 charnsitr/Shutterstock.com; p. 18 adike/Shutterstock.com; p. 19 gritsalak karalak/Shutterstock.com; pp. 20, 21 sciencepics/Shutterstock.com; p. 22 Naeblys/Shutterstock.com; p. 23 Alila Medical Media/Shutterstock.com; p. 24 LightField Studios/Shutterstock.com; p. 25 (inset) QAI Publishing/Contributor/Universal Images Group/Getty Images; p. 26 solar22/Shutterstock.com; p. 29 Sergey Novikov.

Printed in the United States of America

CPSIA compliance information: Batch #CW19GS: For further information contact Gareth Stevens, New York, New York at 1-800-542-2595.

CONTENTS

Words in the glossary appear in **bold** type the first time they are used in the text.

THE CIRCULATORY SYSTEM

There are **fluids** circulating through your body all the time! The circulatory system, which includes the cardiovascular and lymphatic systems, is what keeps them moving. The cardiovascular system is made up of the heart and blood **vessels** called arteries, veins, and capillaries. The heart pumps blood, carrying **oxygen** and **nutrients** to, and removing waste from, the body's **tissues**.

The lymphatic system is made up of lymphatic vessels and **organs**. A fluid called lymph moves through the system and helps the body fight illnesses.

THE CIRCULATORY SYSTEM

CARDIOVASCULAR SYSTEM

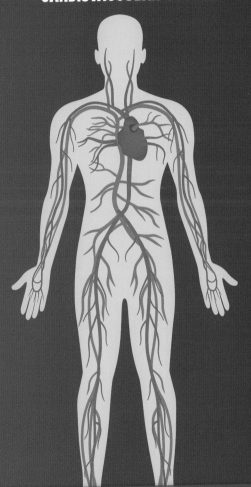

LYMPHATIC SYSTEM

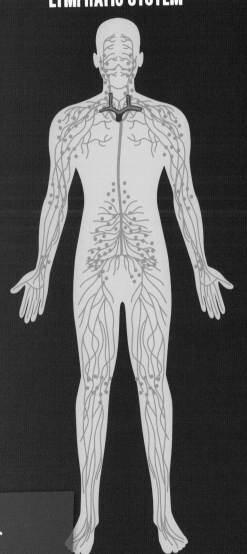

Blood circulates, or moves without stopping, through the cardiovascular system. Lymph circulates through the lymphatic system. It makes sense that these two systems form what is called the circulatory system!

FOLLOW YOUR HEART

BLOOD CIRCULATES ALONG TWO MAIN PATHS!

In the pulmonary loop, blood moves from the heart to the lungs, where it picks up oxygen. It's then carried to the rest of the body in the systemic loop. It drops off oxygen and picks up waste before reentering the pulmonary loop.

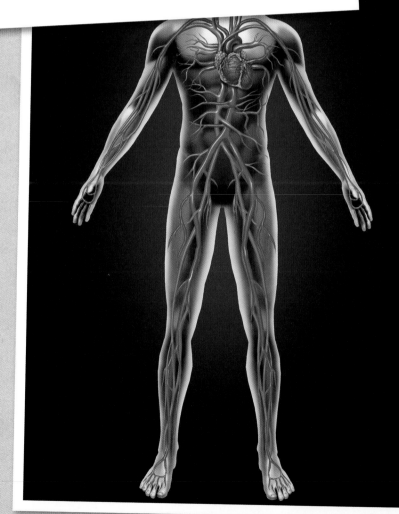

BLOOD CIRCULATION

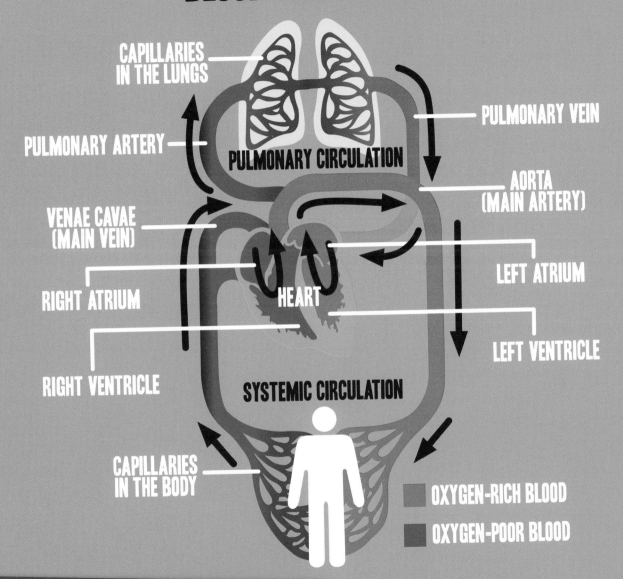

CAPILLARIES IN THE LUNGS

PULMONARY VEIN

PULMONARY ARTERY

PULMONARY CIRCULATION

AORTA (MAIN ARTERY)

VENAE CAVAE (MAIN VEIN)

RIGHT ATRIUM

HEART

LEFT ATRIUM

RIGHT VENTRICLE

LEFT VENTRICLE

SYSTEMIC CIRCULATION

CAPILLARIES IN THE BODY

OXYGEN-RICH BLOOD

OXYGEN-POOR BLOOD

The red shows blood that has oxygen, and the blue shows blood that needs to get more!

THE CENTER OF IT ALL

THE HEART IS A MUSCLE!

Most of the heart is made up of cardiac muscle, a type of muscle found only in the heart. Because the heart beats for an entire lifetime and never gets a break, the muscle needs to be extremely strong!

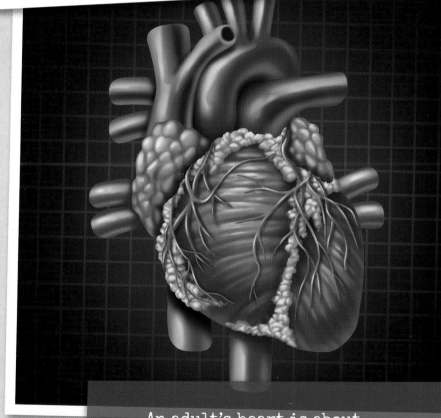

An adult's heart is about the size of their fist.

A child's heart beats faster than an adult's.

THE HEART NEEDS ELECTRICITY TO BEAT!

Your heart is controlled by an electrical **impulse**. A small

amount of electricity tells the heart muscle to contract, or

squeeze together. When the electricity stops, the heart muscle

relaxes and lets go. This squeezing and letting go creates

a heartbeat.

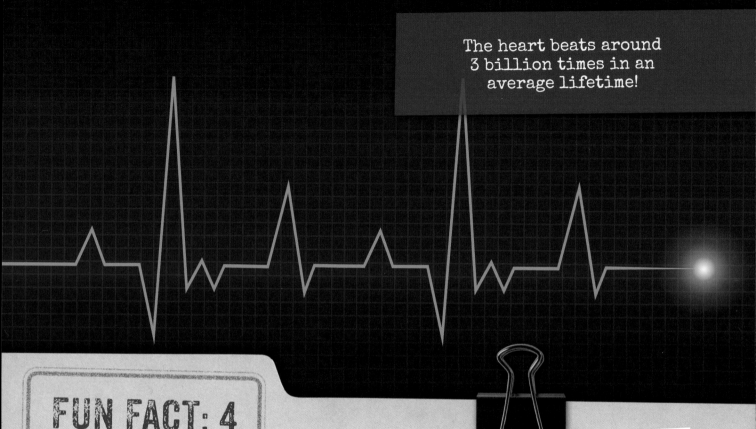

The heart beats around 3 billion times in an average lifetime!

THE HEART BEATS AROUND 100,000 TIMES A DAY!

When at rest, an adult's heart usually beats between 60 and 100 times per minute. This can change if a person is sick, exercising, or having strong feelings about something. It also changes depending on the size of a person's body.

BLOOD FULLY CIRCULATES THROUGH THE BODY IN ABOUT 1 MINUTE!

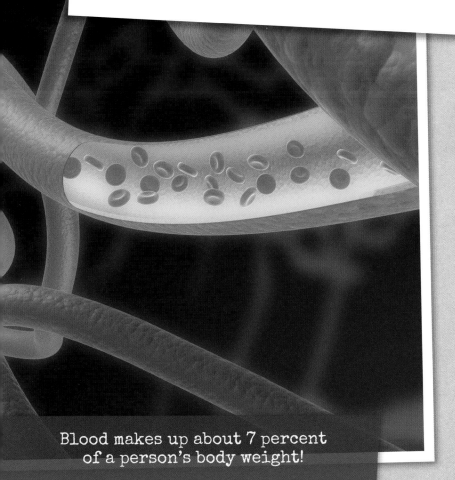

Blood makes up about 7 percent of a person's body weight!

The average adult has about 10.6 pints (5 L) of blood in their body. It travels through the pulmonary and systemic loops about 60 times every hour. That's about once every minute!

11

INTERNAL PIPES

THE AORTA IS ABOUT 1 FOOT (0.3 M) LONG.

The aorta is the largest artery. It carries oxygenated blood, or blood with oxygen in it, away from the heart. The body's smaller arteries are all connected to the aorta. They help carry oxygenated blood to the rest of the body.

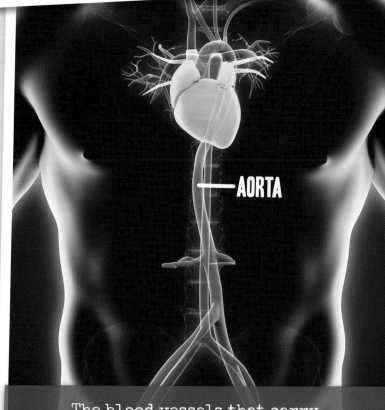

—AORTA

The blood vessels that carry oxygenated blood away from the heart are called arteries.

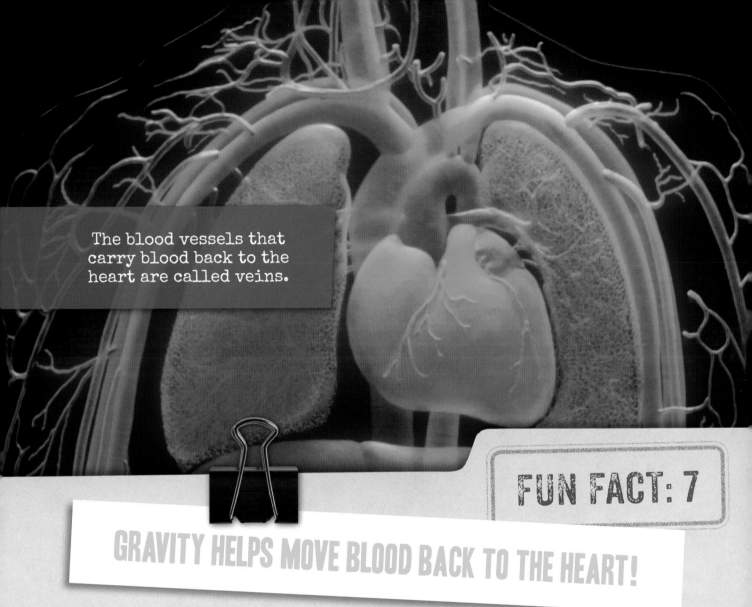

The blood vessels that carry blood back to the heart are called veins.

GRAVITY HELPS MOVE BLOOD BACK TO THE HEART!

The body uses **valves**, pumps, and muscles to move blood through the body back to the heart. In the upper part of the body, **gravity** helps!

13

SOME BLOOD VESSELS ARE THINNER THAN A PIECE OF HUMAN HAIR!

Capillaries are the smallest blood vessels. They're where oxygen and nutrients are **exchanged** with wastes, such as carbon dioxide.

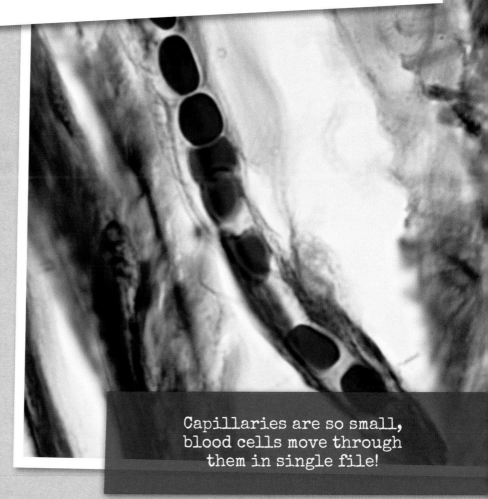

Capillaries are so small, blood cells move through them in single file!

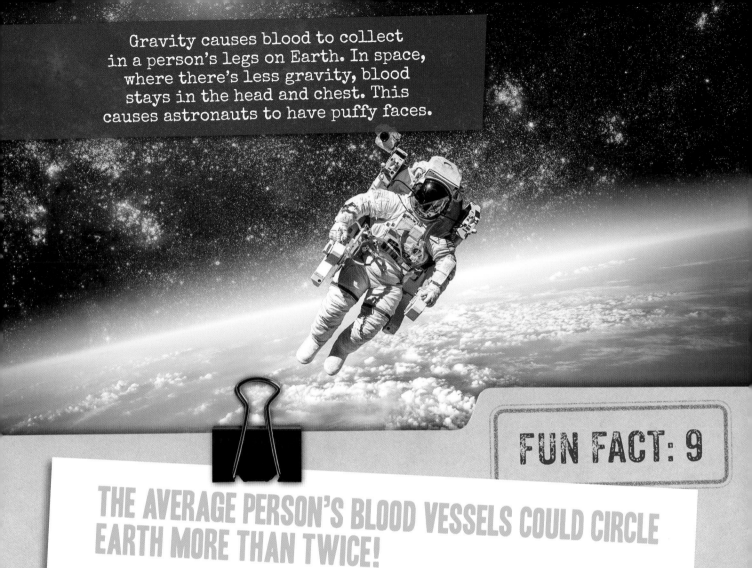

Gravity causes blood to collect in a person's legs on Earth. In space, where there's less gravity, blood stays in the head and chest. This causes astronauts to have puffy faces.

FUN FACT: 9

THE AVERAGE PERSON'S BLOOD VESSELS COULD CIRCLE EARTH MORE THAN TWICE!

If you were to place someone's arteries, veins, and capillaries end to end, they would stretch for over 60,000 miles (96,561 km)!

Your face might get red when you run around, but don't worry! It's just your body trying to cool off.

FUN FACT: 10

BLOOD VESSELS KEEP YOUR BODY THE PERFECT TEMPERATURE!

When the body gets too warm, blood vessels near the surface of the skin grow in size so heat can escape. When the body is cold, these blood vessels get smaller to keep heat in!

HARDWORKING BLOOD

BLOOD COMES IN TWO SHADES OF RED!

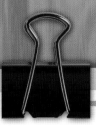

Even though blood is red, veins look blue because you're seeing them through your skin.

Blood in the arteries is bright red because it's full of oxygen. Once the oxygen has been used, blood turns dark red as it moves through the veins back to the heart and lungs.

17

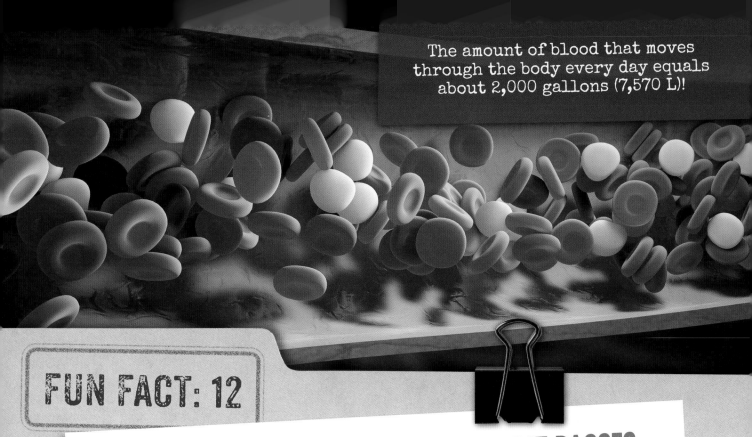

The amount of blood that moves through the body every day equals about 2,000 gallons (7,570 L)!

BLOOD PLASMA IS RECYCLED EACH TIME IT PASSES THROUGH THE HEART!

This means the heart is pretty busy! Plasma is the liquid that carries blood cells through the blood vessels. "Whole blood" is made up of about 55 percent plasma and about 45 percent blood cells.

THERE ARE THREE KINDS OF BLOOD CELLS!

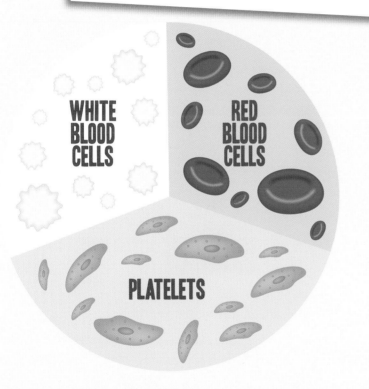

WHITE BLOOD CELLS

RED BLOOD CELLS

PLATELETS

Red blood cells carry oxygen through the body. White blood cells help stop the body from getting sick. Platelets help blood clot, or become thick and solid, so cuts stop bleeding.

Platelets rush to a cut and plug it up to stop bleeding.

19

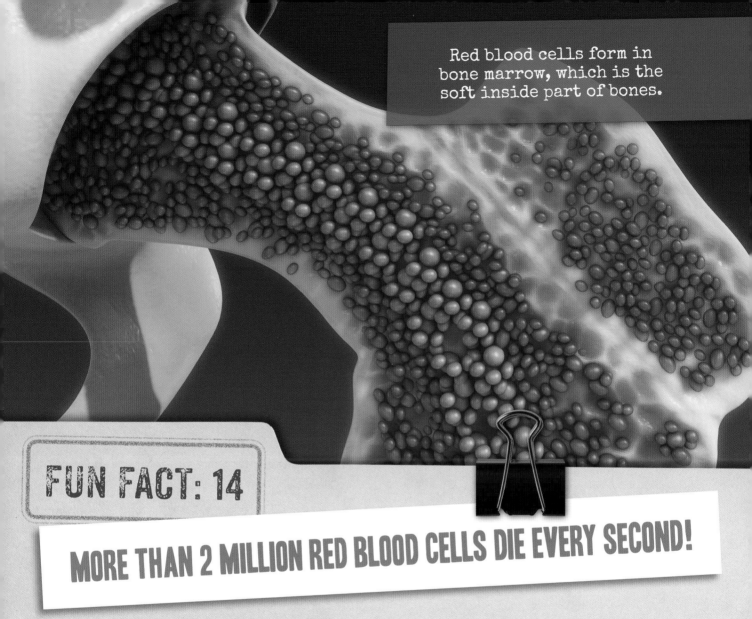

Red blood cells form in bone marrow, which is the soft inside part of bones.

MORE THAN 2 MILLION RED BLOOD CELLS DIE EVERY SECOND!

Red blood cells die every 3 to 4 months. New red blood cells are made at the same rate that old red blood cells die. This means the body always has the same amount of blood.

LOTS OF LYMPH

THE LYMPHATIC SYSTEM DOES DOUBLE DUTY!

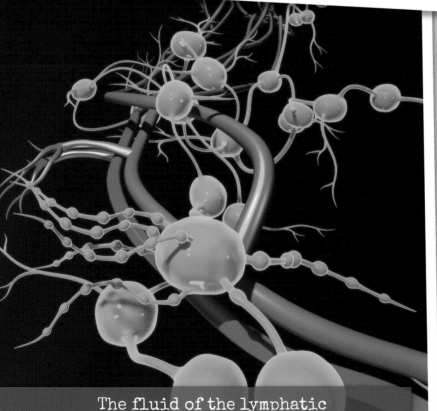

The fluid of the lymphatic system is called lymph. It's a clear liquid filled with white blood cells, which help the body fight off illnesses.

The lymphatic system is part of the circulatory system and the immune system. The immune system is what keeps the body healthy and protects it from viruses and bacteria.

21

THE LYMPHATIC SYSTEM ONLY FLOWS IN ONE DIRECTION!

Lymph bathes the body's tissues. The lymphatic vessels pick up the lymph and carry it up toward the neck. Along the way, the lymph moves through lymph nodes where waste and other harmful matter is removed.

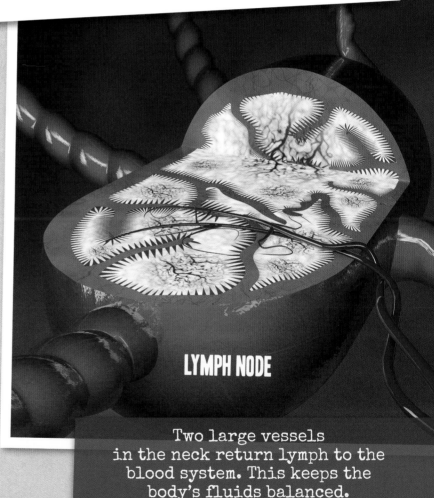

LYMPH NODE

Two large vessels in the neck return lymph to the blood system. This keeps the body's fluids balanced.

LYMPHATIC SYSTEM

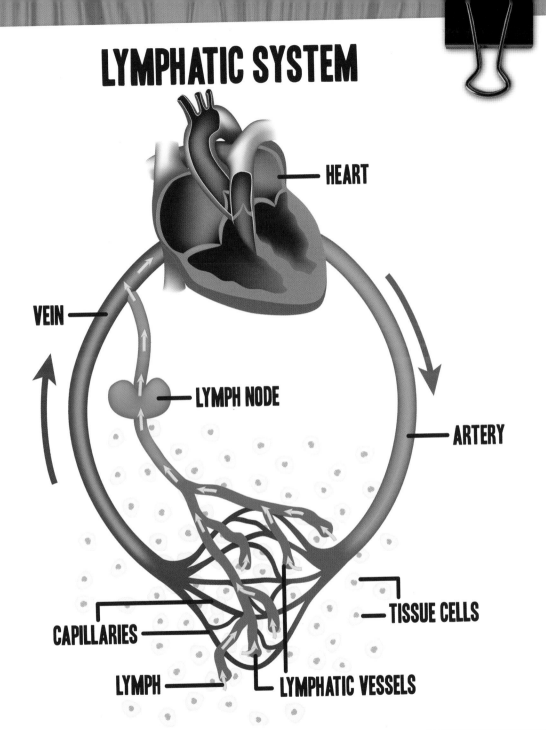

HEART

VEIN

LYMPH NODE

ARTERY

CAPILLARIES

TISSUE CELLS

LYMPH

LYMPHATIC VESSELS

23

CLEAN MACHINE

THERE ARE BETWEEN 500 AND 1,500 LYMPH NODES IN THE HUMAN BODY!

Lymph nodes are located all over the body, but most are found in clusters, or groups, in the neck, armpits, and **groin**. Some parts of the body, such as the skin, don't have many lymph nodes.

Lymph nodes help remove waste, bacteria, and **infections** from the blood. Your doctor might check the lymph nodes in your neck if you feel sick.

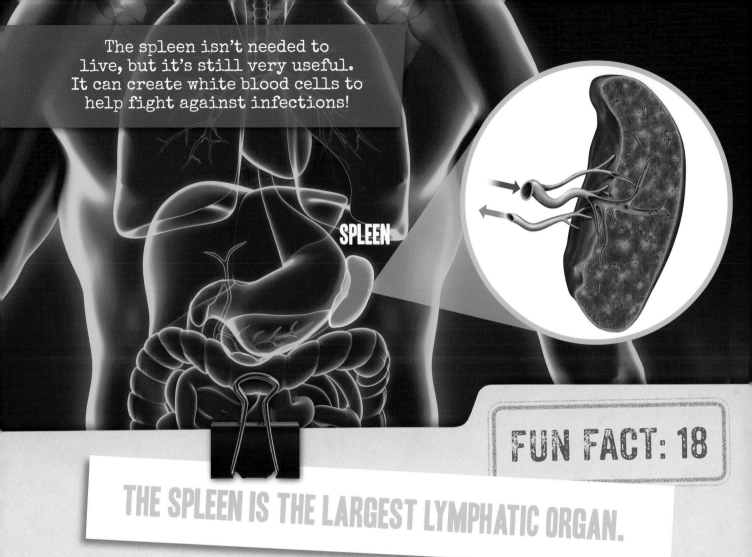

The spleen isn't needed to live, but it's still very useful. It can create white blood cells to help fight against infections!

SPLEEN

THE SPLEEN IS THE LARGEST LYMPHATIC ORGAN.

Though it's a lymphatic organ, the spleen cleans blood instead of lymph. As blood passes through it, dead blood cells and bacteria are **filtered** out. The spleen also stores about 8 ounces (0.2 L) of extra blood in case of an emergency.

The tonsils can become infected and sometimes need to be removed.

NORMAL TONSILS

INFECTED TONSILS

FUN FACT: 19

THE TONSILS ARE A BIG CLUSTER OF LYMPHATIC CELLS!

The tonsils sit at the back of the throat and produce white blood cells. They also kill any bacteria or viruses that may come in through the mouth or nose.

THE THYMUS GETS LESS IMPORTANT AS SOMEONE GETS OLDER.

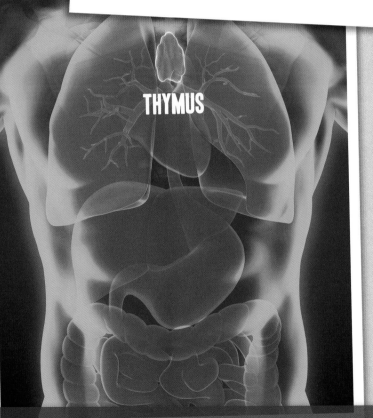

THYMUS

T cells are mostly produced during childhood. The thymus gets smaller and is replaced with fatty tissue as a person gets older.

The thymus is a lymphatic organ found in the chest. It makes T cells, a type of white blood cell that kills bacteria and viruses in the bloodstream. The thymus grows throughout childhood but shrinks as the immune system gets stronger!

27

A HEARTY SYSTEM

The heart is an important part of the circulatory system, but there are many parts to this system—and they all have a job to do! From making sure body tissues have the oxygen they need, to keeping blood clean, the fascinating circulatory system keeps you alive and healthy.

The circulatory system is only one system in your body. Your bones and muscles each make up a system. Your many organs, such as your stomach, are part of other body systems. The human body is amazing!

In order for a body to stay healthy, all its systems need to work together. You can help by sleeping and eating well and getting plenty of exercise!

29

GLOSSARY

exchange: to give something and receive something in return

filter: to collect bits from a liquid passing through

fluid: something that is watery and flows like a liquid

gravity: the force that pulls objects toward Earth's center

groin: the area of the body where your legs come together

impulse: a small amount of energy that moves from one area to another

infection: a sickness caused by germs. Also, the spread of germs inside the body, causing illness.

nutrient: something a living thing needs to grow and stay alive

organ: a part of the body (such as the heart or liver) that has a certain job

oxygen: a colorless, odorless gas that many animals need to breathe

tissue: matter that forms the parts of living things

valve: something that controls the movement of liquids or gases through tubes or vessels

vessel: a small tube that carries fluids to different parts of a person's or animal's body

FOR MORE INFORMATION

BOOKS

Kenney, Karen Latchana. *Circulatory System*. Minneapolis, MN: Pogo, 2017.

Mason, Paul. *Your Hardworking Heart and Spectacular Circulatory System.* New York, NY: Crabtree Publishing Company, 2016.

Walker, Richard. *Human Body*. London, England: Dorling Kindersley, 2014.

WEBSITES

Circulatory System
www.brainpop.com/health/bodysystems/circulatorysystem/
Watch a fun movie about the circulatory system.

DK Find Out! Heart and Blood
www.dkfindout.com/us/human-body/heart-and-blood/
Learn more about how your heart works to keep you healthy.

Spleen and Lymphatic System
kidshealth.org/en/teens/spleen.html
Visit this website for more information about the lymphatic system.

INDEX